P.K. BRISTOL

WALKING THROUGH ANGER

The Essential Guide to Anger Management,
Learn The Effective Techniques on How You Can
Deal With Your Anger Issues Easily

Descrierea CIP a Bibliotecii Naţionale a României
P.K. BRISTOL
  WALKING THROUGH ANGER. The Essential Guide to
Anger Management, Learn The Effective Techniques on How
You Can Deal With Your Anger Issues Easily / P.K. Bristol –
Bucharest: Editura My Ebook, 2020
  ISBN

P.K. BRISTOL

WALKING THROUGH ANGER

The Essential Guide to Anger Management, Learn The Effective Techniques on How You Can Deal With Your Anger Issues Easily

My Ebook Publishing House
Bucharest, 2020

TABLE OF CONTENTS

DO YOU HAVE AN ANGER   PROBLEM?

We see these angry people on TV all the time. The husband and wife, arguing while they're washing dishes, who end up smashing plates full of food all over the kitchen. The angry teenager screaming "I hate you!" at his parents while he smashes his cell phone into the wall and then runs to his room

and slams the door. Even young children get into the act, stomping on toys and throwing tantrums left and right. And then someone usually says something funny, the audience laughs, and the whole incident is forgotten.

What they don't show you on TV is that someone has to clean up that mess in the kitchen. And someone has to pay to replace the plates. They don't show you that the reason the teenager thinks it's OK to scream and destroy his cellphone is because he watches his parents act the same way. And they don't tell you that the reason the toddler is so angry is because everybody else in the house is always screaming and throwing things.

What they don't show you on TV is all the harm anger can do. It has lasting effects on everyone around you. The toddler who is standing in the doorway witnessing the plate-throwing incident between mommy and daddy is learning that, when you're angry, it must be OK to scream and throw things. Mommy and daddy do it. And it must be OK to call people names – mommy and daddy do it all the time.

On TV you don't get to see that same toddler, a few years later, physically attack their third grade teacher or try to poison their fifth grade teacher because they didn't like the grade they got on the math test. You don't get to see that same toddler grow into an angry teenager who takes a gun to school or the mall.

All you see on TV is that someone gets angry and that it's OK to violently express that anger...and then everyone laughs.

In real life, it's pretty easy to recognize when someone we know at work or school, or even just an acquaintance, has a problem with anger. They yell a lot, they throw things, they stomp their feet, they call you names and say terrible things to you, they behave irrationally, sometimes even putting themselves or someone else in danger.

Unlike TV, though, the things they say to you are not funny. They're often very hurtful, things that they would never consider saying if they weren't so angry.

Things that they apologize for later, but that can never be taken back or forgotten.

Their actions aren't funny, either. Breaking plates and destroying property shows a lack of respect, not an appreciation

9

of comedy. In fact, a lot of times, their actions are threatening. Imagine what that toddler in the doorway must really feel. I doubt she's laughing at all the fun mommy and daddy are having. More likely, she's frightened, which means she feels threatened.

We see these angry people every day and we tend to shy away from them. There's no telling what will set them off and we certainly don't want to be around the next time their violent temper erupts. But what if these angry people are right in your house? What if you can't get away from them? Worse yet, what if the angry person is YOU and you just don't realize it? What if YOU are the reason your entire household is always so upset and everyone you love is angry themselves?

Too often we look for scapegoats, we look to others to blame for our bad choices because it's difficult to accept that we ourselves may be the problem. The way I look at it, when the same issues continue to arise, when you often find yourself at the center of turmoil in your personal and professional life and you always arrive at the same outcome, for example your co-workers keep their distance from you and you find the same is

true at home and your spouse and family do the same thing then perhaps the problem isn't purely coincidental. If you find that you keep getting the same outcomes and reactions from people in your life, then it could be you. It's what you're doing that you're not aware of. This should be a wake up call that you need to change. The sooner you can recognize this in yourself and that you need to change, the quicker you'll have your life back on track.

Just remember, if you keep getting the same reactions from people in regards to your behavior then you need to take a good long look at yourself and change some things. Wake up and observe other's reactions to you, why do they treat you in a certain way?, what is it you are doing for people to treat you in this manner? Observe not only what you say to others but how you say it and how they react in response. You might find that you come across angry or have an aggressive tone when you speak without even realizing it.

ASK YOURSELF THESE QUESTIONS

1. Are you frequently angry? Not just disgruntled or negative. But angry to the point that you can feel yourself getting red in the face, you can feel your blood pressure rising, and you want to strike out at something or someone.

2. Does your anger last for long periods of time? If your child spills his milk at breakfast are you still yelling at him about it when you pick him up from school?

3. When your boss makes you angry, do you take it out on your family at dinner that night?

4. Does the least little thing set you off? Do you get angry when the paperboy misses your porch and the paper lands in the driveway instead? Do you allow trivial things that should have no effect on your life to make you angry?

5. Do you find yourself always on the defensive? When someone points out to you that your shoe is untied it's not a criticism, it's an observation. People who have anger issues constantly feel they are being criticized and they become angrier because they feel they need to defend themselves.

6. Do you allow anger to control your life? Do you miss out on enjoying your time with your family because you're just too angry about what happened at work today? Is your job performance suffering because all you can concentrate on is what you should have said during your performance review?

7. Do you use your anger to help you get through life? Do you have to adopt an "I'll show HIM" attitude before you give your boss your best effort? Do you only try your best so you can prove someone wrong?

8. Is your anger too intense? Does your anger feel more like rage, to the point where you can't control it, the point where you couldn't stop being angry now no matter how hard you try?

9. Do you become aggressive and violent when you're angry? Are you the one smashing dishes and cell phones? Do

you strike out at others when you're angry – either physically or verbally?

You may have purchased this guide in an effort to help you deal with an anger issue that's going on in your own home or your own life. And there may very well be a person in your life that has a problem with anger management. If that's the case, then this guide will help you learn to deal with those people.

But if you answered yes to any of the above question, then you may have an anger problem, too. That's not to say that you are causing the anger problems of those around you or that you are even the cause of any anger problem. But somewhere along the line, you have been affected by anger, just like that toddler in the doorway. Somewhere along the line, you were taught that it's OK to express your anger in any way you see fit. In fact, you may even think it's necessary to become violently angry because somewhere along the line, someone told you:

IT'S NOT GOOD TO HOLD YOUR ANGER INSIDE.... LET IT OUT!

But there are healthy ways to express your anger. And throwing things, screaming, stomping around and hurting those around you is not healthy. With this guide, we're going to take a look at just how much better your life will be when you learn to control and manage your anger.

Contrary to what you may think, managing your anger does not mean that you have to go through the rest of your life with rose-colored glasses on. You don't have to become a doormat either. It's OK to get angry. It's a natural, human emotion. But your life, and the lives of those around you, will be much better if you learn more productive ways of expressing that anger when it occurs.

ANGER AND ITS AFTER EFFECTS

In recent years we've heard more and more about anger management, mainly because the effects of anger have become so prevalent in the news. One of the most insidious forms of violence, domestic violence, is on the rise and its cause is directly attributed to anger. Men commit 95% of all reported domestic violence and domestic violence is the number one reason for women seeking emergency medical attention.

Poor anger management is also the leading cause of physical abuse resulting in serious injury or death of children. Researchers found that, in 2004, over 80% of children who were killed were under 4 years old. And Shaken Baby Syndrome, an injury that directly results from a poor ability to manage anger,

affects between 1,200 and 1,600 children every year. In 2004, an estimated 3 million children were found to have been abused or neglected.

Domestic violence is a learned behavior. Children who are abused, or who witness abuse or violence, often grow up to be angry, abusive, violent adults. The cycle often begins with men who have low self-esteem, who imagine the world is against them, and it builds into an all-consuming anger that eventually escalates to violence and abuse. These men become husbands and fathers and pass their abusive and violence behaviors on to their children and the cycle repeats itself.

Poor anger management leads to violence and by either allowing, excusing, or ignoring that behavior, we actually encourage it and allow it to grow. When angry people learn there won't be any consequences for their violent behavior, the violence just gets that much worse. And as the other people in the household see how successful the angry person is, they too, turn to anger to get want they want. Especially since there are no consequences for their poor behavior.

Children who grow up in these angry, abusive households quickly learn that, in order to get what they want, it's okay to destroy things and hurt other people and the cycle continues.

Once caught in this cycle of anger and abuse, it's difficult to escape. The angry abuser commits a harmful act toward a member of his family, either verbally or physically, and then feels remorse for what he's done. Then he becomes angry with himself for losing control, the anger escalates and the abuse happens again. The person who has poor anger management skills often convinces himself that he'll feel better once he "lets that anger out", but does he really?

You might think you feel better when you're in the middle of that rage, but when it's over how do you feel? You probably want to curl up under a rock somewhere. Don't worry though. Just as anger and violence can be learned, so can anger management. The cycle can be broken.

TYPES OF ANGER

There are different types of anger. Different things make us angry for different reasons. Recognizing what type of anger you're experiencing will help you to control it. So before we take a look at different ways of managing your anger, let's try to define your anger first.

Behavioral Anger

People who experience behavioral anger usually confront whatever is making them angry. And it's usually other people. This confrontation typically begins with verbal rudeness and often escalates into violence.

Chronic Anger

These people who experience chronic anger are the people who hate the world, they hate everyone in the world, they hate themselves, and they usually can't tell you why. They're fly off into temper tantrums at the drop of the hat and they're just angry all the time.

Constructive Anger

Often the result of anger management techniques, these people channel their anger in a constructive manner to get the results they want.

Deliberate Anger

Your boss might be a good example of deliberate anger. It's often used as a ploy to control subordinates and it doesn't usually last long.

Judgmental Anger

People who experience judgmental anger often have low self-esteem and they express their anger by putting other people down in public in an effort to try to make themselves look better.

Overwhelming Anger

Exactly what it says. These people are so wrapped up in their anger that they can't take it any more. They often result to destruction or violence, or even physical violence, causing harm to themselves or someone else.

Paranoid Anger

This type of anger is totally without cause. Generally due to low self-esteem, the person imagines that someone is against him and resorts to anger and violence to lash back at their imagined attacker.

Passive Anger

These people typically use sarcasm or mockery as a way to express their anger and they stay away from confrontations and conflict. Which generally makes them even angrier with themselves for not being able to handle the object of their anger directly.

Retaliatory Anger

Probably the most common type of anger, this occurs as a direct response to someone else lashing out at you or doing something that makes you angry.

Self-inflicted Anger

People use this type of anger to punish themselves for something they think they've done wrong. They may cut themselves, or overeat, or even starve themselves.

Verbal Anger

Anger that's expressed verbally, not physically. People who experience verbal anger use insults and criticism to put people down and hurt them psychologically.

Volatile Anger

When something is volatile, it's explosive. Anger is the same way. This type of anger can erupt out of nowhere and can be extremely violent. It often comes and goes without any warning.

These are the most common types of anger. Do you recognize any of them in yourself? As I said, different types of anger occur in different circumstances. And something that made you angry yesterday may not even bother you today. But it's important to understand the different types of anger that you may be experiencing so you'll be able to decide how best to handle each different situation.

THE BENEFITS OF ANGER

It's important that you know you're not alone. Everyone experiences some type of anger every day of their life. And the point of learning to manage your anger isn't to suppress it and completely do away with it, but to learn how to channel it in a positive way to improve your life and your relationships.

While uncontrollable rage and anger can have very negative effects on your life, properly managed anger can also be very positive. For one thing, anger can be very motivational. Think about it. When you're angry with your boss, you tend to work harder to show him he was wrong. When you're angry with yourself for not meeting a goal or accomplishing a task, you try that much harder to get it done.

Experiencing anger is also another way our bodies signal us that something is wrong and that we need to take care of it. When we angrily snatch up our child just as they're about to jet into the street, or we stand up to a bully for a friend or colleague, or when we jump in and help that stranger who is being mugged.

These are all occasions when our anger has spurred us to action in an effort to right a wrong.

Many of the most important changes in society have come about because someone was angry with the way things were and wanted to right the wrong. For example, the Civil Rights Movement and Mothers Against Drunk Drivers and PETA.

If it weren't for outraged activists, we wouldn't have the laws we have that protect children, the mentally ill, people of different religions and ethnic backgrounds, the handicapped and disabled. And the list goes on and on of people who have been helped because someone became angry and decided to channel that anger toward a positive end rather than one of destruction and violence.

The next time you get angry and say or do something you'll feel sorry for, just remember that anger does have it's place and don't beat yourself up about it. Instead of wallowing in guilt and making yourself even angrier, take responsibility for your actions and work on managing your anger instead of letting it manage you.

ANGER MANAGEMENT AT WORK

Up to this point, we've been discussing the effects of anger on your home life, but the fact of the matter is that a lot of people lose their jobs every day because they simply can't control their anger.

Flying off the handle at home is bad enough. Your family loves you and they're willing to stand by you while you learn to manage your anger. But losing control at work can make your superiors begin questioning your decision-making capabilities and you may just end up losing your job.

Before you really get angry and start venting at work, look at yourself from your coworkers' perspective. Will they think your anger is justified, or will they just think you're a raving

lunatic? If you don't think everyone will see it your way, it might be best just to forget about the transgression and move on.

Probably the number one reason that people get angry at work is because they take things too personally. If your boss offers you constructive criticism or advise about your job, it's meant to help you improve your performance. It doesn't mean that he doesn't like you or that he doesn't appreciate your efforts. It just means that he needs the job to be done right and he wants to show you how to do it.

The easiest way to manage your anger at work is to put yourself in the other person's shoes before you fly off the handle. Imagine what you would feel like if you were standing in the middle of the lunchroom and you're boss was yelling at you in front of every one. It would feel pretty degrading.

Or imagine you need to tell someone that they aren't doing the job properly. You wouldn't want someone telling you that you're doing a horrible job. You'd want them to encourage you to do a better job. You wouldn't want to be treated with such disrespect so you shouldn't treat others that way.

THE PRICE OF ANGER

If we're going to discuss the effects of anger in the workplace, we may as well look at the total price of anger, because it effects far more than your job. Although anger can sometimes be a good thing in our lives, it more often than not leads to harmful results, such as road rage, domestic violence, child abuse, physical assault and even murder.

Researchers have found that there are 5 major costs of anger: Your Health

Research shows that chronic, high levels of anger are directly connected to an increased risk for health problems. How often you express your anger and HOW you express it during

periods of emotional distress are significant determining factors in its impact on your health. Stress levels rise, heart rates increase, blood pressure rises. All of these are negative effects and when experienced repeatedly, over an extended period of time, can have disastrous effects on your health.

Your Safety

How often do you drive with pent up hostility? Road rage is an epidemic these days and driving angry behind the wheel of a 3,000 pound car can be dangerous. Driving in anger can impair your judgment and make you an unsafe driver both to you, your passengers and the driver's around you.

Your Self Esteem

While it might feel good when you're in the heat of the moment, expression of anger often leads to feelings of guilt, embarrassment, shame and remorse when you realize that your reaction was probably a little overblown. This results in damage to your self-esteem.

Your Relationship

Frequent angry outbursts, whether verbal or physical or both, can destroy marriages, disrupt families and ruin friendships.

Your Children

The effects of constant exposure to chronic, intense anger can be devastating to your children, often more so than experiencing their parents' divorce. It's not until you see yourself through your children's eyes and the traits they've learned from you do you truly comprehend the far reaching

consequences of your anger. Don't forget that anger is a cycle, our children only mimic what we teach them through our example.

The Workplace

Quality and quantity of production can be severely affected by poorly managed anger in the workplace. Jobs have been lost because of uncontrollable outbursts. Anger in the workplace can also impair judgment and cause you to make poor choices.

Your Time

How often do you see little children get angry over the smallest things? They cry and stamp their feet and invest so much time and energy into reacting and being angry that they often forget what it was they were initially angry at in the first place.

This happens to both adults and children, age is irrelevant. How often do we let anger steal away precious moments? By

being blindsided in fits of rage it can cost us from living the moment and from truly enjoying life.

You'll find that people who live their lives in this way often remember years down the track the anger they felt but forget the great game of golf they played until the anger interrupted them.

THE WARNING SIGNS OF ANGER

If you're reading this guide, you've realized that you have a problem with managing your anger. It's always better to be able to anticipate a problem and head it off at the pass, so here are

some early warning signs you can look for to let you know that you're about to erupt.

Physical signs your anger is escalating:

* Clenching your jaws or grinding your teeth
* Upset Stomach
* Headache
* Rapid heart rate
* Sweating
* Dizziness
* Shaking or trembling

Emotional signs of anger:

* You feel like striking out, verbally or physically
* You feel guilty
* You feel resentful
* You feel anxious
* You feel sad or depressed

* You feel irritated

* You feel like you want to run away

Little Tells To Watch Out For:

* Rubbing your temples

* Pacing

* Getting sarcastic

* Raising your voice

* Acting abusive

* Pounding your hand with your fist

* Begging to yell, scream or cry

These are just a few of the physical warning signs that your anger is getting close to getting out of control. Unclenching your teeth or stopping yourself from pacing certainly won't do anything to help you manage your anger. This is also not to say that any time your palms are sweaty or you have a headache you're experiencing anger.

But, if you are in a situation that is leading to anger, then noticing that you're experiencing these warning signs will let you know that you're about to lose control so that you can do something to prevent it before that happens.

10 BASIC ANGER MANAGEMENT TECHNIQUES

Not everyone who experiences anger has anger management problems. Most people have, at some point in their life, gotten so angry they "see red" as they say, or angry enough to scream or cry. They might even get angry enough to smash a dish or two. But they are also able to get that anger under control and get on with their lives. They control their anger; their anger does not control them. And they don't allow their anger to affect their lives, either. They haven't lost a loved one or a job because they can't control their anger.

But you may not be so lucky. If poor anger management techniques are taking a toll on your personal and/or professional life, then put this book down right now and give yourself a pat

on the back for recognizing that you need help and being strong enough to accept it. Managing your anger can be quite a challenge, but, as they say, a journey of a thousand miles begins with the first step.

Take a deep breath and slow down

Many times, when people feel angry, they start moving and working at a furious pace. They speak faster, drive faster, move faster, all in response to the fight-or- flight reaction our body feels as a response to increased adrenaline from an emotional or physical trigger. When you pick up the pace like that, you sometimes forget to slow down and take a look at the big picture. Instead, you jump into that argument with every intention of drawing blood.

The next time you get angry and ready to fight, force yourself to slow down and take a deep breath. Actually, take 3. Breathe deeply, in through the nose, and then exhale slowly through the mouth. The increased oxygen has a calming effect on your nervous system and will counteract that adrenaline that's

rushing through your body that makes you want to kill someone. This will also give you time to calmly asses the situation and find a better way of handling it.

Take a step back

When you're involved in an angry situation, your first response is to jump in and attack. But your best choice is to step back and reflect on what's really happening. Rushing in with an angry response will only escalate the conflict and provoke an even angrier response. Let the other person have their say and try to understand their point of view. Seeing the big picture is much easier when you step back from the situation and the anger that may be inhibiting your communication.

Take a break

Sometime, it might take more than just stepping back from the situation. Stress may be igniting several peoples' fuses to the point where everyone is angry and confused. If you're at the

point where no one is thinking clearly, it may be best if everyone just go there separate way for awhile.

Depending on the size of the problem and the time necessary for all involved to cool off, you could meet back up in 5 minutes or reschedule the discussion until everyone has had time to get their emotions under control.

Watch an instant replay

When you start feeling your anger ready to erupt, take a look back at what led you to this state. Was it something someone said? Or is it something that happened in the past that's triggered by a current issue? Give yourself time to admit you're upset and then to figure out why. Once you know why you're upset, it will be easier to come up with an effective and appropriate solution. You may have to replay the scenario a few times to understand why it's making you so angry. Once you come to the root of this anger, you may even eliminate it entirely.

Walk a mile in their moccasins

The next time you start to get angry because your child didn't make his bed the way you want it made, put yourself in his position. Literally. He's much shorter than you and he doesn't have the dexterity yet, to handle making those perfect hospital corners. Did your husband forget to pick up milk on his way home from work? Walk a mile in his moccasins and see if you'd remember to stop at the market after the day he just had. If nothing else, put yourself in their shoes to see what it would feel like to be on the receiving end of your anger day in and day out.

Take a walk

If necessary, go for a walk for a few minutes to work off your anger rather than take it out on someone else. Take your dog for a walk, stroll around your neighborhood or head out to the loading dock to stretch your legs. Exercise of any kind relieves stress and your anger will drain along with the stress. Avoid walking like you're heading off to kill someone though. Walking rapidly may actually feed your anger, especially if you

42

continue brooding while you're walking. I know it sounds trite to tell you to stop and smell the roses, but you'll find that if you do, or look up at the sky, or notice the birds in the trees, your anger will almost instantly evaporate simply because you've redirected your thoughts.

Once your anger dissipates, you'll be better able to find a solution to whatever the problem is that made you angry to begin with. Regular exercise is a wonderful way to eliminate stress and if you can get in the habit of walking several times a week, you may notice your bouts with anger getting fewer and fewer.

Talk to a friend

When you're in the middle of an anger-inducing situation, talk to a friend. Call them on the phone, send them a letter, or chat on the computer. Meet up for coffee! Anything that will let you get your negative emotions into words. If a friend isn't available, write it down in a journal. Ann Landers even suggested just writing your negative thoughts down on a piece of paper and then throw it away. Just the act of getting it out and venting is often enough to dispel the anger and let you get on with finding a solution.

Be ready to listen to your friends, too, when they have a problem. You'll not only help them, but it will give you a different perspective on your own problems, sometimes making you thankful that your problems aren't as bad as theirs.

Learn to listen

When you feel yourself getting angry with someone, listen to what they have to say. Many people SAY they listen but all they're really doing is keeping their mouth shut while the other

person speaks, and plotting what they're going to say next when it's their turn again.

We have two ears and one mouth for a reason. We should listen twice as much as we speak. Really listen to what the other person is saying, even if they're also speaking in anger. Be sure you understand their viewpoint. If you have to, ask them to clarify a point for you. There's no sense in getting angry or violent if you don't know why you're getting angry or violent.

Get a pet

If you can't keep a goldfish on your desk at work, then get a puppy, or a kitten, or even a guinea pig for home. Even if you CAN keep a goldfish at work, get a pet for home. A pet gives you a sense of companionship and responsibility.

Interacting with a pet helps relieve stress and calm your nerves. Relieving stress and anxiety helps control anger outbursts and managing your anger becomes more important when you have someone dependent on you to look after.

Put on a happy face

The next time you feel yourself getting angry, just smile. I know, it sounds stupid. But try it now. Smile and hold it for 5 seconds. It's hard to stay upset when you're smiling, even if it's forced. It's even harder for someone to stay upset with YOU if you're smiling. Not only will you calm yourself down, you'll diffuse all the other anger, too, with something as cheap and simple as a smile.

DIFFUSE YOUR ANGER WITH POSITIVE
SELF TALK

I'm sure you've had it happen where someone says or does something first thing in the morning that makes you angry for the rest of the day. Maybe even the next 2 or 3 days. Your entire day or week is shot because of one minor misstep that someone took that has made you angry and now you can't get over it.

Your mind is constantly roiling with comebacks and "should have said's". You imagine what would happen if you had said THIS, and what would he think if you said THAT.

And it eats away at you, constantly, until you're exhausted from the argument that's going on inside your head and you're so angry you're physically ill.

This chaotic conversation you've been having with yourself is called Self-Talk and we all do it. Just not necessarily to the

extent that you are. This constant replay of "what ifs" and "should have saids" is what keeps your anger smoldering. In fact, you're actually fanning the flames into what will soon become a raging inferno.

By changing your self-talk, you'll be using a very popular anger management strategy. The general idea is that our inner thoughts, the words we speak to ourselves, have a great impact on how we feel. If our self-talk is angry or antagonistic, it's very probably that our anger will increase. Meaning, if we continue that battle in our heads, we'll only end up losing.

By the same token, if we change our self-talk into something more calming and soothing, we're more likely to experience less anger and feel less violent. For example, instead of thinking, "If he says that one more time, I'm going to explode!", try thinking, "Take a deep breath, stay calm, I can get through this".

To help you better understand the power of positive self-talk, consider the impact the other person's words have on you when you're angry. Haven't you ever been really angry and then the other person says something that goads your anger even

more? And then think of a time when you've been really angry and a friend has told you to take a deep breath and calm down. Just having that sympathetic person tell you to calm down usually helps. You COULD have remained angry, but you chose to stay calm and handle things appropriately simply because your friend was there to offer you calming advice.

Recognizing and understanding the importance of your friend's words will help you to understand that, even though your friends are not always around, you always have the option to take that step back and calm down. Sometimes, you just need someone to tell you that you have that option. And if there's no one else around, you have to tell yourself. The key is, you have to pay a little more attention and start replacing that negative self-talk with positive words of encouragement.

Although changing your inner conversation that you have with yourself might not be easy at first, the more you practice the better you'll get at it. So practice, practice, practice and keep in mind just how powerful your words can be and that they hold the key to managing your anger.

DIFFUSE YOUR ANGER WITH ASSERTIVE COMMUNICATION

Do you find yourself getting angrier because you can't communicate your feelings in a way that they can be understood

50

by the other person? And then, when they can't understand you, you get even angrier and communicate even worse, which makes you even angrier? It's a vicious circle and one from which you can easily escape if you learn to practice Assertive Communication.

Assertive Communication involves expressing your feelings honestly in order to achieve your goal. Usually, when you decide to assert yourself, instead of just being a pawn in the anger game, you feel better about yourself, even if your goals are not achieved. You walk away from the confrontation knowing that you put forth your very best effort to communicate your concerns to the other party. By using Assertive Communication techniques you avoid those feelings of guilt and remorse that so often occur after an angry confrontation.

Using Assertive Communication techniques can be a little tricky at first because you must react differently to each new situation. Behavior that applies to one person or circumstance won't necessarily apply to the next. Each situation is different and there are times when a passive response might be your best course of action. There may also be times when an aggressive

response is called for but most of the time, assertiveness is the solution.

Always be true to yourself, your own thoughts and feelings and beliefs and avoid criticizing the other person's thoughts, feelings, or beliefs. These are aspects of their being that can't be changed and you'll only put the other person on the defensive if you tell them they can't possibly be feeling something. How do YOU know what they're feeling?

When communicating assertively, think in terms of I-messages. An I-message expresses your feelings without making the other person responsible for them. An I-message doesn't judge the other person or blame the other person. And an I-message never tells the other person what he should think or feel.

In order to successfully use assertive communication you need to know exactly what you want to accomplish, you need to take personal responsibility for your own actions, you need to be able to communicate effectively with the other person and you need to be willing to listen if they become defensive.

The basic steps involved in communicating assertively are:

Give a brief, non-judgmental description of the behavior you want the other person to change.

John, I really wish you would take Timmy to his softball practice on Saturdays. Tell the other person your feelings.

I feel very stressed, now that Janey is involved in soccer, too, and I just can't seem to find a way to get them both to their practices and still feed the baby her dinner.

Tell them something concrete and tangible that explains how this feeling is affecting you.

Last Saturday I was in such a rush I dropped Timmy at the soccer field, took Janey to the softball field and lost the baby's bottle somewhere in the car.

Describe the behavior that would be satisfactory.

If you could take Timmy to his softball practice on Saturday, then I could get Janey to soccer and still have time to take care of the baby, too. Plus, you and Timmy would have some father-son time together.

Anger Management
How To Control Your Anger To Get The Most Out Of Your Life

Notice that you haven't accused John of being a lazy bum or shirking his duties. As a result, he's more open to listening to what you have to say. You've told him how you feel and you've given him a tangible example of the effect his behavior is having on your life. Simply telling someone you feel sad or angry or blue, doesn't tell them anything. You can't see or touch a feeling, so some people have difficulty grasping your meaning.

By giving them a tangible example of how their behavior is affecting you, you give them something that they can hold in their hand and look at and examine, to see how they can fix it.

This type of communication takes practice on your part. It would be very easy to tell John that you'd like him to quit watching football for a couple of hours on Saturday and take Timmy to ball practice. But what you really want is for him to take Timmy to practice. Whether he watches a ball game or not has nothing to do with it. If you throw that comment in there, though, you'll just put him on the defensive.

SERVE THEM A SANDWICH

When you're angry, have you ever found yourself getting even more angry and frustrated because you can't seem to explain what's bothering you? Do you feel like the other person isn't really listening to you or that they're not trying to see things from your point of view? When this happens, you probably end

up raising your voice, talking even faster, and maybe even becoming verbally or even physically abusive. Unfortunately, this makes it even more difficult for the other person to understand you and because you're now verbally attacking them, they don't even want to try anymore.

Or do you go the opposite direction and just try to keep all of your anger bottled up inside? It's not worth the hassle of trying to get someone to understand you, so why even bother? The whole problem with that is that eventually, like a balloon that keeps filling up with more and more air, eventually your anger will explode.

However, if some of the air is periodically released from the balloon, the pressure is relieved and it never reaches that point of explosion. In the same manner, if you use assertive communication to get your point across, you'll avoid having your anger explode, too. Assertive communication is an anger management technique that involves using honesty and effective communication to explain your feelings in a non-hostile fashion.

The most difficult part of using assertive communication is to express your thoughts or feelings in such a way so you don't

56

make the other person angry or defensive. After all, to be able to control your own anger, it's sometimes necessary to be able to control the other person's angry response. If you can keep the other person calm, it's often easier for you to remain calm, also.

The reason this is so difficult is because generally, people don't like to be criticized. When you tell someone they did something wrong or what you don't like about their behavior, or how they hurt your feelings, you can very often put them on the defensive. And someone who is on the defensive is just one small step away from anger.

One of the best ways to use assertive communication is a technique called the Compliment Sandwich. The meat of the sandwich, your complaint or criticism or concern, is sandwiched between two pieces of bread which are compliments or positive feedback. In order to make the other person feel less defensive and more receptive to your complaint or criticism, begin by offering them a compliment, a piece of bread. Then, follow it up with your main concern, the meat, and finish with another compliment, the other piece of bread.

As an example:

John, you're one of the best salesmen I have on the team. You're numbers are phenomenal! (First compliment/Positive feedback)

But the guys in accounting tell me you haven't been turning your reports in on time and it's causing them to get behind with the auditors. (Concern)

I'm sure you've just been busy with all your new clients and I just wanted to let you know the guys in accounting could really use your help. (Second compliment/Positive feedback)

Now, of course you could have gone at it in an entirely different manner. You could have cornered John in the break room, in front of several other employees and let him know just how angry you were that the auditors have been calling you at home every night looking for his reports. And then John would have gone on the defensive because he feels he's already working his tail off by getting you all these new clients. And

eventually one or both of you would have ended up exploding and possible even losing your jobs.

But, as you can see by the example, the Compliment Sandwich made it possible for an important message to be conveyed in a non-hostile manner. Neither party is on the defensive, no one has any anger bottled up and waiting to explode, and a positive outcome will be the result.

There are a few key considerations to keep in mind when using the Compliment Sandwich. First of all, your compliment has to be real and genuine. As difficult as it may seem with some of the people you have to deal with, you need to be able to come up with at least 2 sincere compliments. You may have to think on this for a while, but there are generally at least two nice things you can say about a person.

Your compliments should also be related in some way to the message you're trying to convey. For example, I complimented John on his increase in clients. Had I complimented him on his tie, he wouldn't have seen that I understood he had been doing a lot of extra work lately. He might have gone on the defensive thinking that I didn't

59

understand he'd already been putting in a lot of extra effort. It's also necessary that your compliment be related so that it doesn't sound contrived. I wanted John to know that I appreciated his hard work but that I still need to have his reports in on time.

The next time someone hurts your feelings or makes you angry, try offering them a Compliment Sandwich and you may be pleasantly surprised at the results.

DEALING WITH AN ANGRY CHILD

Dealing with an angry child can be one of the most difficult aspects of parenting. You may find yourself constantly battling, and constantly exhausted, after repeated battles that you eventually win only because you hold the trump card - "Because

I said so". But winning a battle of wills with your child simply by tossing your ace on top doesn't leave you with a feeling of confidence in your parenting abilities. After the battle is over, you often feel ashamed of yourself for handling it that way, and guilty for showing your child that you're angry.

Many of us, as children, are taught that it's wrong to get angry, that being angry is bad, or, that if we're angry, we must have done something to deserve it. These kind of mistaken beliefs are what make it so difficult for us to deal with our children when they become angry.

So, the first step toward helping your child manage his anger is to understand that it's OK to be angry. It's a normal, human emotion. What you need to do is help your child learn how to channel that anger in a more productive way.

There are many things in our adult lives that make us angry. Standing in line at the grocery store, mistakes at work, flat tires on the freeway. We need to remember that there are many things in our children's lives that make them angry, too, and allow them to feel those feelings of anger, but show them acceptable ways of expressing it.

62

Children generally respond with anger because they feel helpless. Their chubby little fingers can't seem to make that bow in the shoelace. Or they can't figure out how to button their coat. They also feel like they are helpless against you. They have to go to bed when you tell them, they have to eat their veggies. They have no control, therefore they feel helpless.

But, to understand why one child becomes angry and then quickly skips off to the playground while the other child becomes violent takes a little more time and effort. What caused the outburst? The thing to remember is that, in adults, our angry seems to be more a generic emotion. But in children, anger can be triggered by embarrassment, loneliness, anxiety and hurt. Children respond with anger in these situations because they feel helpless to understand them fully and helpless to change them.

It's important to remember that anger isn't the same thing as aggression. Anger is a temporary emotional state caused by frustration, while aggression is often an attempt to hurt someone or destroy property. Let your child know that it's OK to feel angry, but aggression is definitely not allowed.

Dealing with a child's anger and aggression requires that you first find out what they are feeling. Ask them what happened or why they are feeling the way they feel. But explain to your child that anger is OK and then let them know that you get angry too and here's how you handle it.

EIGHT TIPS FOR ANGRY CHILDREN

Acknowledge and reinforce positive behavior - "I'm glad you shared your train with your brother." "Thank you for hanging up your coat." "I like the way you handled your brother when he took your doll away." "You were really patient while I was on the phone. Now, what was it that you wanted to ask me?" This lets your child know that you appreciate and expect positive behavior.

Ignore inappropriate behavior that you can tolerate – Nagging while you're on the phone can be dealt with with positive reinforcement – Thank you for waiting while I was talking on the phone. I'm finished now, so what did you need? and then ignore the behavior that you don't like – ignore your

child's interruptions while you're on the phone. Now, you'll probably say that if you ignore them they only scream louder. But, they scream louder because they know they will always get your attention. Ignore their inappropriate behavior and they'll get the message.

Just Say "NO!" - Your child needs limits and you should set those limits and enforce them consistently. Don't say no all the time though. Say yes every now and then, when it's appropriate, and let them know why it's OK for this one time.

Your child needs exercise – When we adults get angry, we sometimes need a physical outlet for that anger. We jog, we take a walk around the block, we go to the gym and hit the stairmaster with a vengeance. Your child needs an outlet, too. Let them run around and make a little noise for a while to let off some of that steam. They're in danger of erupting just as much as you are.

Also, keep in mind that a hug is a powerful emotional band-aid for a child. Don't hug your child, though, to make the anger go away. Hug him to let him know you understand why he's angry and that you take it very seriously.

Show interest in your child's activities – Attention and pride can often make it easier for your child to deal with negative emotions. When he does experience failures and frustration, knowing that you love him and you're proud of him will make these negative feelings much less significant to your child. Sometimes children express anger in an aggressive way to attract attention from their parents. If they already have your attention, then won't need the aggressive behavior.

Use humor to diffuse anger – Humor lightens any stressful situation, even for kids. Don't use humor to ridicule your child, though, use it to make light of the situation and put it into perspective. "I know you're angry at that little girl for calling you names, but doesn't it make you wonder just what a purple jammy jaws LOOKs like!?"

When situations change, tell your child directly – If you normally let your child play his drum in the living room in the afternoon and you all of a sudden send him to his room he's going to get angry. But if you explain to him that you have a headache and that, just for today, you need him to play quietly

in his room; you can diffuse that anger and also teach him a lesson in compassion at the same time.

Use all your parenting skills – If your child is in the middle of a tantrum that he's unable to stop on his own, pick him up and restrain him. Not only for his own safety, but to let him know that it's OK to step away from the situation if need be. If you have to bargain with your child to get him to stop screaming, then do it occasionally. As adults, we reward ourselves at the end of a long, hard day. Your child deserves a reward, too, sometimes.

Most of all, remember that your child learns his anger management techniques from you. If you curse when you're angry, so will he. If you throw things when you're angry, you can bet he will, too. And if you strike him in anger, he'll repeat the cycle with his own children. Teach your child from a very young age how to handle his anger and you'll be better preparing him for his future.

HOW TO HANDLE YOUR ANGRY TEEN

It happens almost over night. One night, you're reading them a bedtime story and they adore you, and the next night they're a teenager and they hate the fact that you even exist! Welcome to Teenage Anger. You're not the first parent to experience it, and you certainly won't be the last.

First, you need to understand that your teen's anger isn't directed at you personally. Teenagers these days have a

tremendous amount of stress from sources that were unheard of when we were kids. Texting and Facebook alone are enough to drive anyone crazy. Not to mention the physiological changes your teen is going through.

You need to handle your teen's outbursts a little differently than you handle your toddler's though. Let your teen know that, while it's alright to express anger, aggression is unacceptable behavior. And then stop thinking about yourself. Stop wondering why your teens are disrespecting YOU, stop worrying about why they only ignore YOU. Start putting yourself in their shoes and consider all of the pressures they're facing from school and friends and their own bodies.

Once you stop worrying about how they're treating YOU, you can step back and see more of what they're actually going through. You'll be able to communicate with them, to talk WITH them instead of AT them. You're relationship probably won't be like any of those storybook relationships but you'll be helping your teens learn how to handle their anger just by showing them how you handle yours.

SOME FINAL TIPS

As I said earlier, you've made a great first step just by admitting you need help and purchasing this guide. Here are a few more tips to help you learn how to manage your anger.

Count to 10

There are two reasons this works and no one ever mentions the second reason. The first reason, of course, is that it gives you time to calm down a bit and come up with an appropriate response when someone says or does something that angers you. Better to count to ten and remain, than to blow up like a cannon.

But the second reason this looks is because, if you take the time to slowly count to 10, if all you're able to think of is an angry or abusive comeback, think how stupid you're going to look at that point. For example, if someone says, "You're UGLY!", and then you have to slowly count to ten before you say , "Oh Yeah? Well. "

Think how foolish you're going to look having to take all that time to come up with a response. Better to just keep your mouth shut and let the situation diffuse itself at that point.

Once you've calmed down, express your anger – It's healthy to be angry, it's the way you express it that counts. Do walk away or do whatever you have to do to avoid abuse and violence. But do come back after you've calmed down. Don't keep your anger inside.

Think before you speak

I realize that during the heat of the moment it's difficult to stop and think to avoid saying something hurtful. If the situation is that far gone, you need to get up and leave anyway. But, if

you know you're going to have a confrontation and that it may get a bit tense, write down what you want to say beforehand and stay on message. Practice Assertive Communication techniques.

Identify Solutions

Instead of focusing on whatever happened that made you angry in the first place, work with the other person to try to come up with a solution.

Let go of that grudge

It's unrealistic to expect that someone is going to do exactly what you want them to do all the time. At some point they will do something to make you angry.

Learning to forgive the other person will help you both.

Learn to relax

Learning relaxation techniques to help you relax and de-stress will help you control your anger when it flares up. We discussed breathing earlier, but you can also use a relaxation

73

technique called visualization to picture yourself in a relaxing setting or to picture a relaxing scene. Self-talk is helpful, too. Repeating phrases, such as "Take it easy" "Take a deep breath", can help you overcome your anger when it starts to get out of control. Other proven methods of relaxation include, yoga, journaling and music.

SHOULD YOU TAKE AN ANGER
MANAGEMENT COURSE?

Some people have a difficult time even admitting they have a problem controlling their anger. Others admit they have a problem and they want to resolve it, but wanting to and being able to are two different things. Learning to control your anger is a huge task and for some people, it's one they can't accomplish on their own. A person with anger issues may be committed in their heart and mind to make a change, but without a push to take the first step there won't be any positive results.

People who need that little nudge often just need to know that they're not in this alone. They're not the only person who ever had a problem with anger. These people often need the help

and support of a group of people, with similar problems, who will support and encourage them in the fight to control their anger.

An anger management course might be just the thing for you if you need additional help and encouragement while you're learning different techniques to control your anger. These courses are designed to help people, in a group setting, where there will be plenty of other people who share the same problems and experiences. Anger management courses may take a full day and sometimes they're weekend retreats.

But throughout these courses, people are taught useful techniques for managing their anger. They're taught how to deal with their frustrations and emotions and how to discover the triggers for their outbursts. There are many lessons you can learn when you attend an anger management course.

And anger management courses aren't only for adults. There are programs and camps for children, adolescents and teenagers, as well. These courses for younger people are interwoven with interesting, age appropriate activities that will teach your child valuable life lessons regarding all their

emotions, not just anger. They'll be in the course with other children who are also experiencing the same anger issues and they offer each other support and encouragement.

An anger management course may be the thing you can do for yourself and your loved ones, to help you combat your anger issues. It can be exhausting and overwhelming trying to deal with emotional issues by yourself and members of your family won't have the necessary training and knowledge to help you help yourself. Attending and anger management course let's you know that there are people who care about you who are qualified to help you overcome this huge obstacle in your path. And in a group setting, you'll have the help and support of others who are in your same situation who also want to see you succeed.

If you're interested in attending an anger management course, you can get information from your doctor or check with your local mental health organization. You can also find several anger management related services on the Internet.

When you start looking for help with your anger issues, you can be prepared by:

Identify your triggers

Start keeping notes of the things that set off your anger. Whoever you work with will ask you about this and this will just save you some time in the process. But being able to identify what causes your outbursts will help the therapist determine what type of anger you're experiencing so they can determine the best way for you to manage it.

Pay attention to physical signs

Keep a list of the signs you notice as your anger is rising. For example, do you feel nauseous, are your palms sweating, are you clenching your jaw?

Make a not of emotional signs that you notice as your anger is rising, too, such as feeling like you want to yell at someone or feeling like you want to strike someone.

When you do find someone who you want to work with, all of this information will help them to help you that much quicker.

For your mental health, the mental health of your family, and to finally break the cycle, it's imperative that you get help in learning techniques to help you control your anger.

Congratulations, you're now on your way to living the life you truly deserve, the life that anger has been keeping you from.

If you still feel it difficult to control your anger following this course then it's important that you seek out professional help. The root cause of your anger could stem from medical or deeper psychological issues that are outside the scope of this eBook. In this case, consult your medical practitioner because you needn't be alone.

Printed by Libri Plureos GmbH in Hamburg, Germany